The dog with 9 lives
and my other wonderful pets

For children everywhere

Front cover, illustrations, and writing by Angela Edwards

A book that tells you nineteen true stories of my wonderful pets

First edition: January 2025

Published in the United Kingdom
by
Imparto Publishing
impartopublishing.com

Distributed internationally
by
Lulu Press Inc.
Raleigh, North Carolina, USA
lulu.com

ISBN 978-1-910537-69-5 Electronic
ISBN 978-1-910537-70-1 Printed

Copyright © 2025 Angela Edwards

Comments and corrections welcome to
angela@impartopublishing.com

A word from Angela:

This book has been made for all young pet lovers everywhere.

Initially, I just wanted to record the adventures of my little Yorkshire Terrier, who really had nine charmed lives. Having done that made me realise how wonderful my other pets had been and what an impact they'd had on my life.

So, after writing about the 'nine-lives' adventures of my Yorkie, I carried on writing about the lives of my other pets up to the present day.

It has been a real 'trip down memory lane' for me and has given me so much pleasure recalling the wonderful pets that I have been lucky enough to own. They have all given me fun, affection, companionship, and much more.

 I hope you, as readers, will get as much pleasure from reading my book as I have enjoyed while writing it.

Introduction:

About Pepé, the inspiration for this book

What can I say... Pepé, a little bundle of furry black-and-tan fluff, was only eight weeks old when I scooped him up in my hand, wrapped him in a mohair scarf, put him in a 'Size 6' shoe box, and took him home.

Little did I know what adventures he would have and how he would enrich my life.

Love from Angela.

By the way, I have provided spaces on pages 118 and 119 for you to draw and crayon or paint your own loving pets. Just have a go and have fun! (Don't forget to write in their names.) Why not photograph your drawing using your phone and send a copy to me at angela@impartopublishing.com

Chapter 1 – Pepé, the dog with 9 lives

1. Life number one. Visit to London.

This is a true story comprising nine sections about my little Yorkshire Terrier, Pepé.

On the day I left my old job, as a hair stylist in a top London Salon, to start my own salon in West Sussex, I bought this most adorable little Yorkie!

He was only eight weeks old and very intelligent. He was so full of pep that it seemed to me a perfect name for him would be Pepé.

Just a couple of pounds in weight, he could sit in the palm of my hand and sleep at night in an empty shoe box with a woolly mohair scarf to keep him cosy and warm. You can see him in his "Size 6 Shoes" box on the front cover of this book!

His coat was silky and beautifully shiny, and on the advice of the breeder,

I used to bathe him every ten days. It paid off because he always looked immaculate and never minded being handled.

I was so proud of him that I decided to take him up to town to show him off to my old work friends; it was his first proper outing, having just finished his puppy injections.

You have most likely heard of the saying, "a cat with nine lives". Well, my little black and tan Yorkshire Terrier wasn't a cat, but he certainly had nine lives.

He used up his first 'life' on the day that I took him to Helena Rubinstein's hair and beauty salon situated in Mayfair—the smart and most fashionable part of London's West End—where I had been working for the past nine years. I had been apprenticed there and trained as a professional hair stylist.

Oh dear! Pepé slipped out of his collar.

Pepé and I travelled on the underground 'tube' railway from home up to London. He seemed to quite like this experience, sitting on my knee and looking with great interest at every passenger getting on and off the train.

I had bought him a black patent leather collar and lead, and he was lapping up all the admiring attention of his fellow passengers. The only time he was a little nervous was on the escalator, so I slipped him inside my coat, and he peeped out of the neck so as not to miss anything.

When we reached the street level, he was keen to walk, and so he trotted along beside me all the way down famous Bond Street and around into Berkeley Square in Mayfair. I kept glancing down, and there he was right beside me, not seeming to mind the hustle and bustle of all the elegant people on the Mayfair pavements. I had hold of the black patent lead, and we were moving along in style through the busy crowds. It wasn't until we reached the entrance of the salon, and I bent down to pick him up, that I discovered the black patent collar had slipped off!

His little head must have come out, and in fact, he had walked all the way down Bond Street on his own, just following me!

You can imagine what a shock I had, especially thinking about what might have happened if he had dashed out under a car!

A hot, sweet cup of tea, which we both loved, was the best thing for us.

I must say, though, looking back on my little furry friend's "life number one", it was more devastating for me than for him, as he thoroughly enjoyed the rest of his visit, being fussed and patted by all the Mayfair staff. And, once back home, he spent most of his time being cuddled on the laps of the various clients whose hair I happened to be styling!

Little did I know at the time what a character this little dog was going to be!

2. Life number two.
Saved by the vet.

Life settled into a lovely pattern with my little fluffy friend.

Every day, we would arrive at my hair and beauty salon, and as I started doing the hair of my list of clients for the morning, he snuggled down on their laps for a cuddle.

As the day progressed, Pepé would watch for hair rollers that accidentally fell on the floor and would pounce on them, tossing them into the air and then, as they fell, would roll on them. We had to save some, especially for him to play with, and at the end of the day, I had to remove them from his fur before we could go home!

One day, while flinging the rollers about in the usual fashion, Pepé discovered a handbag under a chair. Naturally, he had to examine it carefully, and as it was open, a quick sniff around was the thing to do.

Oh my! Pepé found the painkillers.

There were all sorts of objects inside, and in one corner, a little cardboard box, a bit flat but just the right size for tossing about, and it added variety to the rollers. This was brilliant for chewing until the box got a bit wet and soggy, and what was inside tasted rather bitter and thus had to be spat out!

All this spitting and smacking of lips made everyone stop their work to investigate. What horror struck us when we discovered that the box was a packet of painkiller tablets, and it was impossible to guess how many Pepé might have swallowed!!

Emergency procedures followed and after a telephone call to the local vet an immediate visit was arranged. The lady vet was wonderful and administered a mouth wash and thorough examination reassuring me that it was highly unlikely for a dog to swallow these tablets as they tasted so bitter. What a relief that this little bundle of furry mischief had come to no harm. Life number two had passed.

3. Life number three.
A ride in a taxi.

The incident with the painkillers had happened in the springtime; the summer had now arrived, and we had all worked ourselves into a nice daily routine.

Pepé was still playing with the rollers, but the clients' handbags were now safely stowed away up on shelves.

One particular day was very hot, and it seemed the right thing to do to curl up in the corner and have a sleep—Pepé, that is, not the clients or the staff. Several happy hours had been spent like this when suddenly the peace was broken by a gnashing of teeth and a leaping about in the air—Pepé, that is, again, not the clients or the staff.

At first, it was very amusing to watch, but as we all laughed, one astute person said, "Wait, something is wrong." We all looked and, to our dismay, saw that Pepé had been trying to catch a wasp which had, apparently, stung him on the tongue, which was by now beginning to swell alarmingly!

No time to waste! Another trip to the vet was called for. However, this time, the staff members including myself were so occupied attending to the clients that no one could leave!

So, as it was an emergency to obtain treatment to stop the tongue from swelling any further, a taxi was called. You can imagine the driver's face when he realised that his only passenger was to be a DOG— and a Yorkshire Terrier at that! However, when he heard what the emergency was, he entered into the serious spirit of it with great dignity. Also with great difficulty, I think, as Pepé insisted on sitting on his lap!

Thankfully, in those days long ago, before seat belts were required, the roads were much quieter. Safely settled, the taxi driver and Pepé sped away and left us to our work.

The atmosphere in the salon was now tense and silent, and everyone was worried about poor little Pepé.

Off went Pepé with the taxi driver!

The minutes seemed like hours, and eventually, when the silence was broken, everybody simultaneously said, "I wonder how he is getting on?" Then, just as we were deciding to phone the vet, the taxi pulled up outside. The driver got out and came into the salon, carrying Pepé very lovingly in his arms.

It appeared that in the short time they had spent together, Pepé, instead of sitting on the driver's lap, had snuggled inside his coat. You could say this had had quite an effect, and the man had been completely bowled over by this lovable little dog.

By now, the antidote the vet had administered was beginning to work; the tongue was returning to its normal size, and Pepé, feeling drowsy, settled down to sleep it off in his favourite corner of the salon. We paid the driver and thanked him profusely for being so kind and caring in what could have been a life-or-death situation! He told us it had been an honour, and as he drove off, we breathed a sigh of relief. Life number three had just been spent.

4. Life number four.
At a photo-shoot.

With daily brushing and a bath every ten days, Pepé was, by now, looking very handsome. One of our clients was an author, and having noticed how well-groomed young 'Pep' was looking, she said that it had given her an idea. She was currently writing an article each week for a girls' magazine, on

'How to look after your pets.' Featuring in it was her own pet—a very impressive, very large two-year-old Great Dane named, Henry.

The theme was that Henry would meet 'doggy' friends each week, thus introducing different breeds for the children to read about. As the piece she was writing was in the form of a strip cartoon, real photographs were used, with bubble captions coming from the dogs' mouths. When this was all explained to me, it sounded most interesting. Consequently, it was arranged that Pepé should be taken along to the local photographer to have his picture taken with Henry, and an appointment was duly made.

We arrived early for the session and were shown into the studio, which had a table with a cushion on it, and beside which was a stool. The photographer was very jolly and, on telling us that he regularly took pictures of Henry, appeared to be quite excited at the prospect of this new assignment. We sat and waited in an armchair in a corner of the studio, and Pepé, by this time, was trembling in anticipation as to what was going to happen. I think he must have thought it was some kind of new vet.

Stand-off between Pepé and Henry.

Then the door opened, and in came Henry, followed by—or should I say, "dragging in"—my client, the author!

In the studio with us were many portable lights and umbrella arrangements of the kind that I believe are commonly used in professional photography. Henry, who seemed very keen to get on and have his photo taken, had not noticed either Pepé or me sitting in the armchair.

But Pepé had seen Henry! And, without any warning, sprang into action and leapt up onto the table, growling and barking in a pose of attack! My heart jumped into my mouth because Henry was enormous and, with just one bite, could have swallowed Pepé whole. Pandemonium ensued as we chased around the room, bumping into the apparatus, the photographer only just managing to catch the lights as they fell to the ground.

You can imagine our amazement when we all managed to calm down, only to find Pepé still up on the table, barking and growling with such dominance. Poor Henry was terrified of this furry firecracker! We all laughed, and Pepé, having established that he was completely in charge, very graciously sniffed noses with Henry.

As no damage had occurred in the studio, the result was that some lovely photographs were taken with Pepé, of course, totally unaware of how, once again he had narrowly spent another 'life' and lived to do it all over again.

5. Life number five.
Encounters with Prince

It soon became apparent that Pepé thought he was the most important, if not the *only* dog in the world. Not that he didn't like other dogs; he was always initially happy to meet them. However, after a few minutes of friendly greeting, the growling and snarling would start, with Pepé telling the world that he was in charge.

The size and breed made no difference to 'Pep', who knew no fear. The amazing thing was that all other dogs, after a few protests, took the submissive role and backed down.

How I wish I had known this on the first occasion that Pepé explored the backyard at the salon.

My salon was situated on the High Street, and around the corner was a sub-post office, both premises sharing a red-brick-walled backyard. Also sharing, was Prince—a very handsome and large Alsatian belonging to the sub-postmaster.

The first time the back door was opened, young Pepé bounced out into the yard and straight up to what was standing on guard in the middle of it— Prince, the enormous Alsatian, whose hackles were rising.

Poor Prince did not know what to do with Pepé.

Speechless with shock and horror, we watched as Pepé, unable to reach the Alsatian's nose, walked straight underneath him and out the other end, sniffing all the way as if to say "Well, what have we got here?" We, by this time, were trembling with fear but not for Pepé, who had now decided to come back the same way to the nose end. Poor Prince—whom later we found was a real softy—was so bewildered that he trembled with anxiety, wondering whether and where this little dog might just take a nip.

Well, I think you will agree that this was, again, another 'dice with death' which, luckily, did have a very happy ending because both this handsome and good-natured Alsatian and this plucky, fun-loving Yorkshire terrier, soon became great pals.

6. Life number six.
Saved by the brakes.

By now, young Pepé was maturing into a truly handsome dog himself and was extremely intelligent. Fortunately, he had learnt many commands and acted on them with obedience and speed and, indeed, pleasure.

When out walking in town or city areas, we adopted a routine which we always adhered to. As we approached the curb, I would say, "Sit, wait!" And, if the road was clear, "Over!" It developed into almost a game, with little Pepé knowing the procedure so well that he would sit and wait simultaneously at the edge of the road even before, or as I spoke the words.

However, one day, without any warning whatsoever, he took it into his head to cross the road on his own. What a shock we had!

We were in the middle of the lovely little village where my parents-in-law lived. Parking places were available on either side of the wide high street and, as we always used the spaces on the same side as my in-laws' cottage, Pepé would usually get out of the car with us and walk the short distance from the car to their front door without his lead on.

But this day was different, for as we got out of the car, Pepé decided to wander the opposite way across the main road on HIS OWN!

"SIT! WAIT!" I shouted, and he did!

A car was coming down the street, and how I did it, I will never know, but I managed to scream out at the top of my voice, "SIT! WAIT!" Pepé looked horrified as he heard my screaming instruction, but he had been schooled so well in these commands that he did *exactly* as he was told—even though in the middle of the road.

Looking even more horrified was the lady motorist, who by now was fast approaching. I could have cheered for joy—in fact, I think I did—as, seeing the situation, this almost-petrified lady fortuitously steered her car right over the top of my little dog without running him over and without even touching a hair of him.

As soon as was possible, she stopped her car and ran back to where I was. I had quickly snatched up Pepé, who had remained sitting trembling in the middle of the road.

"Is he alright?" she cried. "Yes," I replied, "you were brilliant!".

What a relief to us all! But I couldn't help thinking, as I strapped Pepé safely into his harness and lead, *this must be another life to notch up!*

7. Life number seven.
A surprise swim

The glorious summer of 1968 went on and on, and there was nothing we enjoyed better than a day at the seaside whenever possible.

Pepé was not very keen on swimming but loved dashing up and down on the edge of the water after a ball, as do most dogs.

There are several beaches along the south coast, but the one with the most sand is West Beach, Littlehampton. This beach had to be reached by a short ride on a little ferry across the mouth of the river Arun. On this particular day, which had passed superbly, Pepé was destined to spend life number seven. He had a wonderful zest for life and had been bouncing about on the beach, chasing everything in sight and thoroughly enjoying himself. We, on the other hand, had relaxed in the sun, eating a delicious picnic of cold chicken and salad followed by fruit and a little scrumptious chocolate. Wonderful!

It was late afternoon, or more like early evening, and the tide was going out. We had packed our picnic and beach things ready to go back to the car via the ferry. Now, as we strolled along the water's edge, Pepé was one beach ahead, leaping over the breakwaters with great confidence as he came upon each of them.

We had been discussing that it was time to attach his lead to the harness he always wore, so we started calling to him.

But he was having a marvellous time, and there was always 'just one more breakwater to jump'!

Pepé leapt over the breakwater straight into the sea!

Unfortunately, he had not realised the one he had just reached was the last

one before the mouth of the river! This was a river that had been dredged deeply and was very busy as a number of yachts sailed up and down to and from Chichester harbour.

With terror in our hearts, my husband, Richard, and I rushed to the edge of the final breakwater over which we had just seen Pepé make a flying leap. We looked over fearfully as it was now almost dusk, and the river's currents swirled fiercely as it flowed out to sea.

With tears in our eyes, we looked out in vain. Then, suddenly, right below us, we saw Pepé doing the 'doggy paddle' in about half a metre of calm water at the river's edge! Being so tiny, he must have jumped over but fallen straight down into the calm, shallow edge of this fast-flowing river. What amazing luck! And even more, there was a hand-over-hand iron-rung ladder about seven metres away towards the mouth of the river.

While Richard climbed down, I coaxed Pepé to swim towards the ladder. Thankfully, Richard grabbed the harness and hauled our bedraggled little bundle to safety.

This time, it really was almost a life spent.

However, with Pepé all wrapped up in a beach towel for warmth, we caught the ferry back but did not return straight to the car. Instead, we went into a nearby pub where Richard bought us both a brandy to help us recover from the shock. Even Pepé, at first trembling with cold and fear, seemed to relax and warm up as we drank our small brandies. Being cuddled by us gave him a lot of comfort. Once safely back in the car, he snuggled up on my lap and finally went to sleep.

8. Life number eight.
Lost in the car park

Lives numbers eight and nine are linked because one follows on from the other and, fortunately, did not get used up until after we had had a few years of calm, blissful happiness. In this period of time, we had produced two wonderful sons, and when the eldest, "Mark", was three years old and the youngest, "Alexander", just a few months old, Pepé decided that it was time for another adventure—in fact, two—as I mentioned at the beginning of this paragraph.

I was out shopping with the boys and Pepé one afternoon, and it turned out to be very dull and gloomy. As it looked like it was going to rain, we hurried back to the car park, and I quickly got everyone in the car. Pepé was, as usual, the first in, and the pram last. It was a detachable one, and the wheels had to go into the boot.

While I was stowing the wheels, Pepé decided to slink out of the car and sniff around on the grass verge of the car park. It was impossible, of course, to see this with my head stuck in the back of the car boot. Thinking everyone was safely tucked in, I drove off, homeward bound. Some fifteen minutes later, as we pulled up in the driveway, I sensed that Pepé was not in the car, and my suspicions were confirmed when my little boy said, "Mummy, where is Pepé?"

Pepé was left behind in the car park!

With considerable fear and trepidation, we drove straight back to the car park—but there was no sign of dear little Pepé. Fortunately, there was a car park attendant in a little hut and when we frantically asked, he said, "Yes." He remembered a little dog with a harness running up and down as if he were looking for someone.

Poor old Pepé, he must have wondered what on earth had happened when, after having his little sniff, he had turned around and found we had vanished! The car park attendant told us that everyone had been anxious and, miraculously, a quick-thinking lady had managed to jump on the end of Pepé's lead. She then picked him up and informed all the onlookers that she would take him to the police station! Life number eight had just slipped by.

9. Life number nine. To the rescue

As I mentioned, life number nine is closely linked to number eight and, as the title of this book is, "The Dog With 9 Lives," this is, appropriately, the last 'adventure' of my little Yorkie. They say that a cat has nine lives, but I have never heard it said about a dog!

Well, I now take up the story again from the moment we were in the car park when we realised that Pepé was safe and indeed would be found waiting at the police station. Not a bit of it! You can imagine our dismay when we were told by the police officer in charge that the lady was so delighted with the little dog that she had taken him home.

According to the officer, it appeared that, initially, she was reluctant to give her address and telephone number and rather reluctantly indicated that she hoped no one would come forward to claim their lost dog! I was angry when I heard this and, armed with both telephone number and address, which the police had managed to eventually extract, we roared off in the car to rescue Pepé.

We found Pepe's new temporary accommodation!

The address was not too far away, and soon, we were entering the drive of a big house with a very overgrown garden and lawns only mown along the sides of the driveway. *This house looks a bit sinister,* I thought. Perhaps that was because it was almost dark, but we ploughed on up to the front door. After knocking and ringing the bell for what seemed ages, the door was eventually opened by a quiet, rather guilty-looking middle-aged lady. I immediately asked about Pepé, and looking somewhat sad, she said, "Yes, he's here. Do come in."

I followed her into the kitchen, where there was another older lady with Pepé. He was sitting on a cushion on top of the worktop, eating chocolate! What a time he was having, loving every minute of the chocolate and the attention he was getting. It was a strange feeling to see these ladies obviously upset that I had turned up, but genuinely pleased at the greeting Pepé gave me.

 As I stood there with him in my arms, one paw around my neck, I couldn't help thinking how lucky I was to have such a wonderful pet. Indeed, the only dog I know to have had nine lives!

Important footnote here... Chocolate, as we all now know, is very bad for dogs and should never be given to them to eat.

Chapter 2. My other wonderful pets

Although I started this book with Pepé, he was not my first pet. However, the rest of the pets, in Chapter 2, are in the right order.

1. My very first pets — Felix and Joey

Pets are the most rewarding and enjoyable living creatures that any family can possess, and writing about my little Yorkshire terrier made me think back to my very first pets which I will tell you about now.

On my ninth birthday, my dad came home carrying a cardboard box, which he handed to me as he and my mum sang, "Happy Birthday". I excitedly looked inside the box and found a great deal of straw, and nestling within it were two tortoises. One was nearly the size of a dinner plate, but the other could only be compared to the size of a tiny saucer.

They were very peculiar-looking creatures, but I was so thrilled to have them, and my mum and dad were pleased to give me such easy pets to care for. Provided that you have a secure garden that they can't escape from and you give them a little shelter to sleep in, they happily potter about, waiting for the next lettuce leaf to appear.

We were told that some bread mixed with a little water in a saucer was also something that tortoises liked. And that was certainly true of my two tortoises as they 'raced' across the garden to get to the saucer first! I decided to give them names to suit their characters. So, the large one I called Felix because I knew a song in which a character called Felix kept on walking. The little one, I called Joey because, to me, it suggested something small. I don't expect that anyone else would understand either of these choices, but they are the ones I made.

Our garden was quite formal, with flower beds around the edges behind low walls. In front of the walls were crazy-paving paths, bordered by a small, shallow trench with a superbly mown lawn in the centre.

My two slow-coaches, Felix and Joey,

Felix and Joey loved walking about on the lawn but often fell into the trench while trying to cross the path. When this happened, they became utterly helpless as they were lying on their backs and could not turn themselves over. At first, we were amused until we realised what a plight they were in.

So, my dad made little wooden bridges at various points for them to use, and, to our amazement, with a bit of encouragement and lots of lettuce leaves from us, they learnt to do so!

This, and the fact that when we called their names, they would come, made us aware of how intelligent these prehistoric-looking creatures actually were.

Felix and Joey loved the sunshine and all the summer months, but like all tortoises, they had to hibernate through the winter. So, as the weather became colder, out would come the cardboard box with lots of fresh straw.

But, before Felix and Joey could be tucked in for their long winter sleep, they needed to have their shells oiled. Because this was so many years ago, the only oil available was olive oil, which one usually bought at the chemist, gently heated, and dripped in one's ear to cure earache problems!

Anyway, poured onto cotton wool, it was perfect for me to rub into Felix and Joey's shells. Once they were nicely oiled and tucked up in the box with a few holes and the lid on, my dad would carefully store the box up on a high shelf in the garage. When spring came, and the clocks put forward, the warming weather would remind us to take the box down from its storage place and bring it into the kitchen.

Gently, we would all open it and carefully take out Felix and Joey, who were just showing signs of awakening but needed to have their eyes bathed with a little warm water. They really seemed to enjoy this procedure and blinked many times as if to say, "thank you". Then it was off into the garden to put out their shelter and reinstate the little wooden bridges that had been packed away for the winter months.

Tortoises seem to be rare nowadays, but in my childhood, they were easily bought at any good pet shop, and for me, they were wonderful first pets.

2 — Roddy

Roddy, my miniature poodle, came to live with us after many requests from me to my parents, "PLEASE may we have a dog?" Poor Dad got so fed up with me asking that, eventually, in early December, he said, "OK, but it will have to be a joint Xmas and a twelfth-birthday present in February!"

So, on the fifteenth of December, a visit to the pet shop saw me coming out with a small ball of black fluff clutched firmly in my hands, in the shape of an adorable little miniature poodle. I am not sure now how we thought of the name Roddy, but we all liked it, and so Roddy it was. In the previous chapter, I wrote about my pet tortoises. Well, you can imagine what excitement there was when Roddy discovered them.

He was fascinated when he sniffed their heads and front legs, which all disappeared immediately inside their shells! At this time of his life, he was only a tiny puppy, so not much bigger than my large tortoise, Felix. It was so amusing to watch this little ball of black fluff sniffing both ends of this large shell, trying to work out what was inside. Eventually, Roddy would give up, and Felix's head, four legs and tail would appear, and he would slowly and sedately walk off.

Roddy would then leap into action, and the whole procedure would begin again. After a while, it seemed that these two pets had come to an agreement, and

Roddy accepted that Felix just wanted to potter about the garden and then withdraw into his shell for a little snooze. It was quite different with Joey, and we were very alarmed one day when we caught Roddy trying to play with Joey as if he were a ball.

This, of course, was because Joey was so tiny. Fortunately for us, Roddy was very intelligent, so after only a few scoldings and purchases of new play balls, he ignored Joey. At the same time that all of this was happening, my best school friend, Anne, had been given a bicycle from her parents, for her Christmas present.

What I will now tell you is that by an interesting coincidence I had been asking for a bicycle and she had been asking for a dog! Neither of our parents had agreed to these requests so Anne and I solved the problem ourselves. She would call for me on her bike and I would take Roddy out with her for a walk. However, when out of sight, just around the corner, we would swap over, so that I was riding the bike, and she was walking the dog.

We did this all the time, and our parents did not find out until one dreadful day when the lead slipped out of Anne's hand, and Roddy decided to run home. Our outings were in the local park, but to get there, we had to cross a busy main road. This, of course, was fine for us because we would walk to the zebra crossing and cross when the red light had stopped the traffic. But the lead slipped, and Roddy made a dash for it! Straight back out of the park gates.

As we chased after him, he just kept on running straight across the road! Thankfully (both for him and for us), there were no cars in the way!

Somehow, he knew where he lived, and we both arrived puffing and panting where he waited, also panting, on the front doorstep. When my mother opened the door, our secret was out, and we received a good telling-off. However, my parents were so relieved that we three were safe that they just bought a stronger lead and told us to be more careful. You may be sure that, as it had given us a dreadful shock, we always were.

By this time, Roddy was fully grown and needed trimming. As poodles have to have their fur shaped in various styles, we gave it much thought and, eventually, decided on the "lamb cut". Although he was a great example of his breed, we knew that we were not going to enter him into any show competitions, so he didn't need the famous "lion cut" with all its pompoms for the show ring. The lamb cut, with a single tail pompom, was just right and, in our opinion, the nicest for him.

After a few fur cuts, and as they were rather expensive, my mother and I thought that we would attempt the trimming ourselves.

Roddy loved to sit up and beg.

Armed with scissors, brushes, and combs, we started on Roddy's back and hind legs. All went extremely well, and we were congratulating ourselves on a good result until it came to the front legs! Roddy did not want us to even attempt them! He repeatedly tucked them under his chin and on no account would straighten them out!

So, after many treats of chocolate with no effect on leg stretching, we had to give up and call the professional dog trimmer to turn a very strange-looking poodle into a handsome one with a proper lamb cut. I must make a strong point here that all this was a long time ago when chocolate was given to pets as a treat, and no one knew that it was poisonous to dogs. In fact, Roddy loved it so much that he would dance around on his hind legs for ages for a reward of a square of milk chocolate. Thankfully, it did him no harm.

When I was fifteen, we moved to a house with a big lawn where he could run around and flower beds to get lost in. But his daily walks were his joy until one day, he was attacked by a huge Alsatian dog.

I was happily walking Roddy on the pavement on one side of the road, and on the other side was a man with a huge Alsatian. Suddenly, it slipped out of its collar and flew across the road, leaping towards Roddy. Well, the man was amazing. He raced over the road, doing a rugby tackle on his dog. At the same time, I yanked the lead and harness, lifting Roddy right up in the air, and just managed to catch him in my arms.

As all this was happening, Roddy was howling with fright, and the Alsatian was growling and snarling. Between us, the man and I succeeded in parting the dogs, but we had all had a terrible shock. The man apologised profusely, and I walked home carrying a screaming, trembling poodle.

Soon after this frightening incident, poor Roddy's fur started to fall out—small amounts at first, then large handfuls.

 A visit to the vet confirmed that the hair loss was the effect of the shock attack that caused the problem. A purple tincture was prescribed to paint on the bald patches, followed by a massage of yellow "flowers of sulphur" powder. This produced a very strange-looking poodle with some patches of black fur and purple and yellow bald areas. Eventually, the treatment did the trick, but as the fur started to regrow, Roddy could not stop scratching and, in doing so, created sore patches on his skin.

Something needed to be done to stop him, so one of the sleeves of my winter jumpers that had seen better days was cut off and made into a polo neck sweater for Roddy, who scratched and scratched till it was threadbare. Then, the other sleeve had to be used. Many sweaters were needed until lovely, lush black fur finally covered his body, and Roddy could go out for his walks without stopping every few minutes to scratch. Poor Roddy!

Many happy years went by, and I left school and started work serving an apprenticeship at a famous Salon in Mayfair, in the centre of London. After finishing my apprenticeship and qualifying as a stylist, I was well-established and decided to get married. That meant I left home and had to leave Roddy with my parents. It was a wrench for me, but the best thing for him as it was his home also, and my parents were really attached to him. A few years passed, and Roddy grew into a lovely, very friendly, old dog. Eventually, at the age of twelve, my much-loved Roddy passed away—a very sad time. But we all consoled ourselves with the thought that, apart from the terrible Alsatian dog attack, he had enjoyed a wonderful, happy life.

3 — Uri and Glenn, the budgerigars

One day, when passing through London's Soho quarter, I noticed an Italian shop selling beautiful wrought iron light fittings and tables. Tempted to look around, I went in and was immediately taken by a really unusual bird cage hanging up amongst the ornate light fittings.

I had not long been married and thought this would be an excellent feature for our new flat. So, without further ado, I bought it. The next thing that arose was the question of how to transport it home as it was far too big and heavy for me to carry and take on the tube train!

At that time, we were living through the 'swinging sixties', where there was only a quarter of the number of cars on the roads compared with today, and the laws were much less restrictive. For example, one could drive into the centre of London and park outside any shop, wherever one wished. So, since I had the following Saturday off work, we sped in the car up to Soho to pick up the birdcage. I feel sure that, at the time, I was not thinking of actually having any birds in it.

However, when my husband fixed it up in our lounge, his first question was, "Are you intending to have a 'budgie' like your grandparents have?" Well, that was certainly an invitation I could not resist as Joey, my grandparents' budgerigar, was amazing. He played patience—a card game—with my grandpa and insisted on helping my grandmother with taking the curlers out of her hair. So, next, off to the pet shop we went, and as we were both working and out of the house a lot, it was decided that two birds should be acquired to keep each other company.

Our recently purchased unusual bird cage was round like the moon, hanging from a beautiful arrangement of ornate, hand-painted, wrought iron flowers.

It was a very exciting time for the country, as space travel was hitting the headlines, and the Russians and Americans were battling it out to be the first to put a man on the moon. Thus, we named our two budgies Uri (the Russian astronaut) and Glenn (the American one).

The birds soon settled in their 'globe', swinging on the swing and climbing the ladder, sitting on the perches and admiring themselves in the mirror. They loved chattering, and when the television got louder, they would get louder too, and the only way to stop them was to say, "Bedtime," and cover the whole cage with a cloth.

A very fancy cage for Uri and Glenn.

When we arrived home from work, we would open the cage door and out they would hop, flapping their wings and flying around the room. It was great fun, as they became extremely tame and loved sitting on our fingers and shoulders as we walked around the flat. Then, one day, we had a real shock when looking in the cage, we found that there were eggs amongst the bedding. Wow! Having thought we had purchased two male birds, we now knew we had a male and a female; no wonder they got on so well!

Consequently, it was 'off to the pet shop' to buy a nesting box. Then, very carefully, we transferred the eggs into it. Success! Three little eggs had been nestled into the box for hatching. Uri and Glenn took turns sitting on them, and after about eighteen days, they started hatching, and we could see these little featherless birds inside the nesting box.

Every day, they became stronger, and eventually, they ventured out into the globe, complete with beautiful feathers, some of them blue and some green. The next step was to teach them to fly by coaxing them to climb onto our fingers and balance while we walked around the room. Uri and Glenn were very supportive, flying alongside us. Their young offspring became quite bold and, one day, as the cage door was nearly always open, hopped to it and, on their own, jumped out.

In the beginning, when this happened without our support, they alarmingly plummeted to the floor. But we had a lovely thick carpet, so no harm was done. After a few experiences like this, the little birds seemed to realise that it was a much better idea to stay in the cage and practice flapping their wings to work up the strength to actually fly, which, within a few weeks, they were able to do.

All this was extremely exciting for us until we saw that they were outgrowing the cage, and we had to do something about it. As it turned out, my excitement had spilled over onto my work pals, to whom I had been relating the budgies' progress.

By now, my friends were asking about the budgerigars every day. We knew that it had been an unusual occurrence to raise baby budgerigars in a home environment, but it seemed to be considered extremely rare.

So, when I announced that we had a problem with 'budgerigar overcrowding' I had a large number of offers to rehome my three feathered babies! What joy, as I personally knew the three work colleagues who wanted to have them. When my friends had kitted themselves out with well-equipped cages and were ready, each one came and collected their new 'budgie' and Uri and Glenn were left, once more, in peace.

I think they were quite happy to pass the time admiring themselves in their mirror, flying around the room, and sitting on our fingers. Our budgerigars did not talk as they had each other, but one on its own makes a wonderful pet as they can be taught to copy words. My grandparent's bird was always saying things like, "Put the kettle on," and "Answer the door." They are not long-lived birds, so knowing this, we were not sad when they passed on after four and a half years because they had a very happy life and gave us so much love, fun and pleasure.

4 – Toby.

Toby was a beautiful tiny little ginger kitten that I bought from one of my clients. At this stage of my life, I was on my own as my husband and I had divorced, and I was running my salon with the help of the manager, Mr Richard, who had been working with the previous owner. He was a very kind and helpful young man and was just about to buy his own cottage so, as a house warming gift, I gave him the little ginger cat whom he named Toby.

Over the years Richard and I became friends, eventually decided to get married, and ended up having a really happy life together.

But going back to Toby, whom this chapter is really about, this kitten turned out to be a real companion for Richard while he was living alone in his cottage.

After our marriage, I moved into the cottage with, of course, none other than... Pepé! Well, you should have seen Toby when they first met. His ginger fur stood up on end and the ears went back as fierce hissing and growling came flowing out of his mouth. The tables were turned for Pepé as, for the first time in his life, he was the one who was afraid. Happily, however and after a few months of giving each other a wide berth, they became good pals and loved chasing each other around the garden.

Toby was stuck at the top of our garden ladder!

Toby had grown into a fully grown tom cat and was the same size as Pepé, so their play sessions were fairly evenly matched.

One day, while we were having lunch, we heard a barking in the garden and, going outside to investigate, we found Toby at the *top* of the ladder that Richard had been using to paint the cottage wall. Pepé was leaping over the garden cuttings that I was piling up on the lawn.

This time, Toby was frightened because, having climbed the ladder, he could see no way of getting down, and so it was left to Richard to come to the rescue. It is no mean feat to climb to the top of a long ladder and safely back down holding a wriggling, large cat in one arm. But it was successfully achieved while Pepé barked with excitement, and I held my breath with relief.

After that experience, Toby restricted his climbing to a large oak tree on the driveway and could often be seen fast asleep on one of the lower branches. He was a very happy cat but too adventurous and, sadly at the age of only three, he was run over and killed on the road outside the cottage. We were devastated. Richard buried him in the garden, where we planted a beautiful red rose.

5 – Monty. What a feline

Monty, our next ginger tom cat, came to live with us as a sort of 'rescue cat'. After the wonderful but short time we had with Toby, a ginger cat was what we were missing.

It was a week day and, after dropping my three-year-old son at play school, I would frequently pop into the local village shop. One morning, while waiting to be served, I heard two little girls in front of me asking if they could put a postcard advertisement in the shop window. The shopkeeper wanted to know what they wanted to sell, and the answer was "Kittens."

Then, to his and my horror, they said, "If we don't get rid of them, our dad is going to put them down the toilet!!" Well, what could I do but say, "I'll have one." The next thing I knew was that I was driving the girls back to their home in order to pick up a kitten. I do not know what I was expecting to see, but after just a ten-minute drive away, the girls shouted out, "We're here." And there, behind some large gates, were rows of long huts that turned out to be full of rabbits.

Next to them was a caravan in which were about a dozen cats, including the mother cat and her kittens. The girls had fetched their dad, and he told me that I could choose any kitten or, indeed, all of them! I would have loved to have done just that, but I knew only one cat was all we wanted. So, as all the kittens clambered over each other, I spotted a little ginger one in the corner, just sitting and watching, and I knew he was the one for us.

The dad scooped him up, gave him to me, and promptly disappeared. The girls ran off playing, and I walked back to my car carrying a tiny bundle of ginger fluff! Then, I had to decide how to drive home with a little kitten loose, sitting on the seat beside me. I realised the only thing to do was to put him inside my handbag, and as he nestled in, I remember thinking how pleased I was that large handbags were in fashion!

Thank goodness it was only a short journey home, but as this had been an impromptu action, I had no basket, food or water bowls, let alone soft bedding for this new little member of our family. Well, it's amazing how easy it is to make things happen if one is pushed to it. A cardboard box with one side cut out, lined with a sweater (with the sleeves tucked in) made a perfect bed. Two odd desert bowls, one for food and the other for water, were all that the kitten needed until we could go to the pet shop and purchase proper things for a cat.

As you can imagine, there was sheer delight and surprise that evening when all the family were playing and stroking this tiny little kitten. Everyone agreed that I had acted responsibly when I heard about the fate of the kittens and even said, "Why didn't you get more of them?"

Decisions then had to be made as to what to name him. I think my husband had been watching a Second World War movie about General Montgomery (who was commonly known as "Monty"), so we all thought it would be a good choice for our little ginger kitten. It turned out to be more than perfect for him, as he grew into a fearless, enormous ginger tom-cat who would take on anything.

Monty grew into a most handsome cat.

He loved hiding—although really only his head was hidden— and then jumping out, giving anyone walking by a playful rugby tackle around their legs. It would be alright if you liked cats because he was very gentle, but Monty seemed to know the friends and relations who were a bit nervous, and he would make a beeline for them. He took pleasure in sitting on their lap and, once there, would fall asleep purring loudly, making them feel guilty if they tried to get up.

He also had a passion for smoked salmon. On one occasion, when he was about three years old, my husband and I were going out to a musical evening and decided to have a little treat of some smoked salmon and a glass of white wine before we left home. While I was getting ready upstairs, Richard put the salmon and wine on the dining table for when I came downstairs. He called to me, and I came down a few minutes later to find an empty plate and a glass of wine!

A bit confused, I went into the kitchen and asked, "Shall I take the smoked salmon through?" "I've already done that." came the reply. "Well, where is it?" was my retort. Then we saw Monty licking his lips and looking very pleased with himself. With the irresistible aroma wafting down from the table, he had been unable to resist and had jumped up onto the dining table and eaten the whole lot!!!

His passion for seafood almost became his downfall as, on one occasion, he managed to get hold of a large prawn complete with its shell! We were absolutely mystified as to how he had done this and utterly alarmed to find him choking under the dining table as we were eating our supper. It was a matter of life or death, and a quick reaction from Richard saved Monty's life as he grabbed the cats back legs holding him upside down, and shaking him until the half- chewed prawn fell out on to the carpet.

Thankfully, this occurrence stopped our beautiful big ginger tom from "stealing", especially any kind of fish food, which we all now knew he adored. So as a special treat I would chop up a prawn and some smoked salmon and mix them with his normal cat food, and he would lick his lips and give me a loud 'meow', subsequently walking away purring to take up his position on the sofa for an after dinner knap!

We, all loved Monty greatly, and he lived with us for twelve more happy years—as you will read subsequently.

6 — Tilly and Tiger

My next 'pet' adventure was when Richard and I were living with our own two boys, Mark and Alexander, in a lovely little cottage in an area called "Snowhill" in West Sussex while Monty was still alive and living with us. He was about twelve years old when we acquired two kittens! They were later to be called Tilly and Tiger as, of course, they didn't have names when they were found!

Can you imagine how exciting it is to find beautiful little kittens? Well, that's what happened to my mother. For some years, she had been feeding a stray cat that had come to live in her large garden. She had given it the name "Kitty" and had tried her best to tame it but was never successful—it was a very nervous cat and would never come close enough for her to stroke.

One day, just as Mum was going into her garden to feed Kitty, she saw the cat walking across the lawn with something in her mouth, so she waited and watched as Kitty proceeded to go back and forth across the lawn, each time carrying something in her mouth. After a while, Mum decided to investigate but couldn't find Kitty anywhere.

Then later, while sweeping an area around the coal bunker, Mum lifted the lid to see how much coal she would need to order (while summer prices were still available) and was very surprised to find Kitty curled up in a corner, nursing four little kittens!

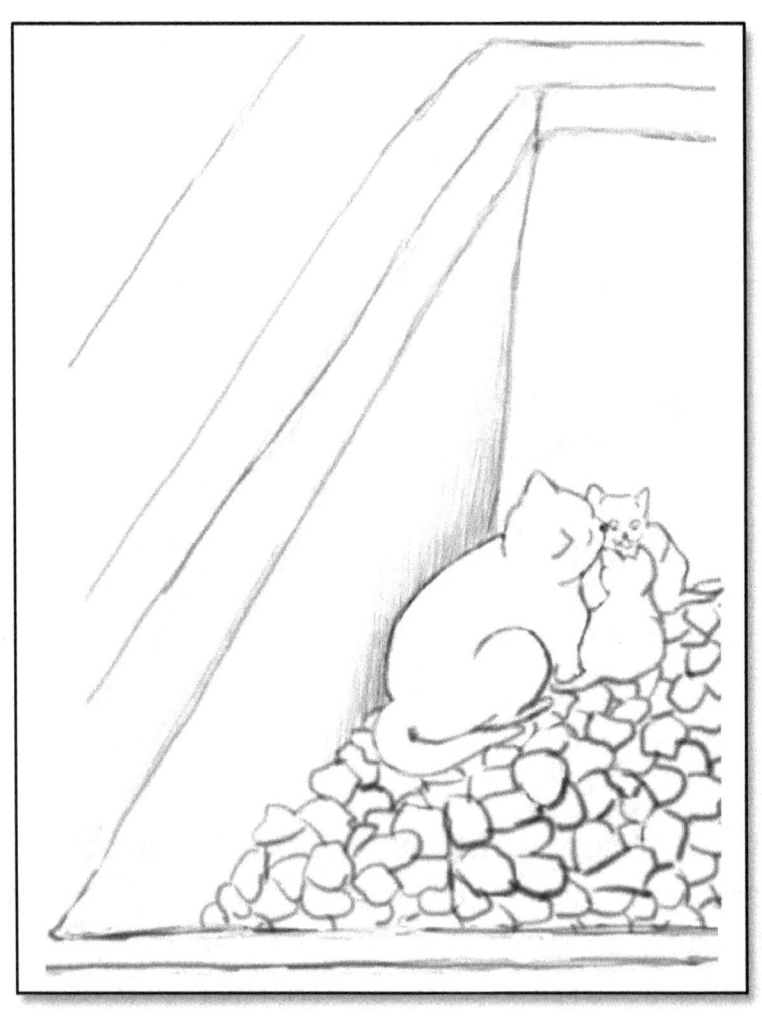

There was Kitty, nursing four brand-new kittens!

When telling me about what she had found, Mum recounted that she didn't know who was more shocked—herself or Kitty!

Next, of course, came the problem of what to do with the kittens when they were old enough to leave their mother, and my mum certainly didn't want another four cats to look after. So, the RSPCA was called, and they said they could only find homes for two of the kittens, and because Kitty was a relatively wild cat, if they took her, they would have to put her down.

Well, you can imagine how upset we all were, but eventually, a decision was made with respect to the kittens. The RSPCA would take two and Richard and I would take two. At the same time, Kitty would be spayed (to avoid her having more babies) and then she would be returned to my mother's garden.

So, that is how Richard and I came to adopt the two kittens that we later called Tilly and Tiger who came to live with Monty at our house.

Monty was very good with the new kittens as he realised that they were no threat to his 'Mighty Ginger Tom' status, being that they were only six-week-old tiny kittens; indeed, he hardly took any notice of them. By the time winter came, they had grown into young adult cats who played happily with us, each other, and sometimes, with Monty in our cottage and garden.

On one beautiful winter's day in January, when the back door was opened, the two young cats sprang out, greatly surprised, into deep snow! Monty immediately retired to his favourite place on the settee as he had seen snow before, but Tilly and Tiger jumped up and down in it, pouncing and chasing with great excitement. It really was "deep and crisp and even" and lasted for days—long enough for my sons to dig pathways through it, which Tilly and Tiger loved running through.

The sledge came out of the garage, too, and the cats needed no persuasion to climb aboard and be pulled around the garden. A few very happy years passed, during which all three cats brought a lot of joy to our family.

Then sadly, one day, Tiger, who had become rather too adventurous, wandered onto the road and was killed! We were all devastated, but fortunately, Monty and Tilly seemed to sense what had happened and kept well away from the road with its busy traffic.

More time passed, and then, one day, panic set in when Tilly disappeared for almost a week. We searched and called and called, but there was no sign of her. Finally, on an extensive search, my husband found her across on the other side of the road; sadly, it seemed that she had just gone away to die. She had not been run over but had simply passed away even though she wasn't old. We think she just missed Tiger too much.

Shortly after losing Tilly, another sad and strange thing happened. Monty—who never usually ventured even as far as the front of the cottage—went missing and was found just a short distance from where Tilly had passed away, and he, too, had died. Unlike poor Tiger and Tilly, Monty had had a long life, but after Tilly disappeared, it seems he went searching for her and, for the first time, crossed the road. Although he was not run over, we think he had been bitten by a snake as there were two puncture marks on his neck. So, there we were—bereft—missing all of our beautiful cats and feeling very sad. The cottage seemed very empty without them. We loved them so much.

7 – Fred, another ginger cat

Life without a cat felt as though something special was missing. Consequently, when one of my clients mentioned that her daughter's cat had produced kittens that needed homes, I immediately put in a request for one. Another excellent reason was that they had mentioned a ginger one amongst the kittens, and after our super ginger tom, Monty, we all agreed that would be the one for us!

So, a visit to my client's daughter's house saw us coming home with an adorable little ginger kitten. The next thing on the agenda was what to call him, and as cricket had almost taken over our family (our youngest son playing for the county colt's team and wanting to bowl like Fred Truman) it had to be "Fred".

Also, another good reason was that this little kitten loved playing with a ball all the time. So, Fred, it was, and this beautiful little ginger kitten was our delight—especially with our cricketing son constantly bowling a tennis ball to him while Fred patted it back. They seemed to have a real bond, which I think developed when our son returned from a cricket tour and fell asleep on the settee with Fred curled up on his chest, also fast asleep. As this happened when Fred had only been living with us for a few weeks, it made the two of them really close.

Fred was elegant, with smooth fur.

Fred loved being with all the family and wanted to join in everything that was going on, and Christmas was his greatest delight. As the boxes of decorations came down from the loft, he would examine them all, and the first one to become empty would be just suitable for a little nap. Eventually, after most of the baubles and tinsel were in place, he would sit on top of our baby grand piano with tinsel draped around his neck, looking like a rather strange but unique Christmas decoration.

He did once try to climb up inside the Christmas tree, but a good telling-off put a stop to that, and he never tried again. Nevertheless, Fred was really enjoying his life with us, and things got even better when a new family moved next door with a very handsome grey Burmese cat called Ashley. He was big like Fred and just as gentle and a bit shy, so he and Fred became great pals as they played together and sunbathed on the flat roof of Ashley's owner's garage.

Then, one day, along came a fearsome feral cat who took no time at all starting to terrorise both Fred and Ashley, chasing and pouncing ferociously on both of them in turn. Fred would fearfully rush back home, charging through the cat flap as fast as he could until, on one occasion, he was not fast enough, and that dreadful feral cat gave him a nasty bite on the base of his tail. After a few days, it turned into an awful abscess. Several visits to the vet followed, and—dreadful news during one of them— the vet announced that if poor Fred's abscess did not heal, he would have to be put down! The reason was that he had lost the use of his tail, and it had affected his ability to balance.

What a worrying time we all had until one day, as the anti-biotics kicked in, Fred's tail began to move, and we knew he would recover. Then more sad news followed as our neighbour tearfully told us that Ashley had also been attacked and regrettably died from his wounds. We were all furious with this horrible feral cat and set about trying to chase it away. No amount of clapping and shooing worked until my husband, Richard, had the brilliant idea of turning the hose pipe on. What a success! No cat likes water, and having to confront a jet of water every time he tried to come into our garden, soon got rid of this nasty wild cat.

We were so delighted as poor Fred had been too nervous to go into the garden. Once he knew there was no more danger, he became more courageous. Over the next few months, we became aware that Fred was searching for Ashley, and we felt sad that we could not explain to him that his friend had gone. Each time he ventured into the garden he ended up looking through the big laurel hedge and then would settle down in it, just waiting.

Quite a while went by, and then one day, my client (from whose daughter we had bought Fred) mentioned that there were more kittens. They came from the same mother as Fred, but a different father. This, we thought, would be the answer to Fred's sadness—he was still searching for his friend. If we had another cat as a companion for Fred, it would cheer him up! So, that's how his half-sister, whom we called, "Bella", came to live with us.

8 — Bella, Fred's half-sister

Bella, Fred's little half-sister, was a ball of tabby-coloured fluff—not at all like her big brother. Both cats had the same beautifully marked tabby mother but different fathers. Fred's father, "Samuel Johnson", was pure ginger, whilst

Bella's father "Barnaby" was a Burmese Blue thoroughbred.

Consequently, there was a big difference between the brother and sister, and it was very interesting for us to watch them interact with each other. At first, when Bella was a kitten, Fred was intrigued with her, but when she would not stop climbing all over him and biting his ears, he got really fed up. During this time, I often visited my elderly mother in Essex to help her with gardening, shopping, and trips to the doctor/dentist/optician, and so on. So, to give some relief to Fred, I decided to take Bella with me as an experiment. It was a great success.

After that, we journeyed together regularly, and she travelled well in the cat basket. The only proviso was that she liked to be sung to, joining in with the occasional very long Meowww!!!

"Daisy, Daisy", "The Wheels on the Bus", or any other song I could manage seemed to satisfy her, and I became extremely pleased on these journeys when she fell asleep, and I could stop singing.

Beautiful Bella.

At that time in my life, I was doing tapestry work, producing beautiful cushions, and I took my work with me to do in the evenings. The canvas was stretched on a frame for easy working, and Bella, being so young and small, took great delight in sitting on my lap and pulling at the wool each time the thread came through. It was amazing how she knew when to stop and wait for the next time the thread came in her direction.

These weekends became a delight for us, as my mother loved seeing this little kitten, and Fred enjoyed a peaceful time back at home.

Then, as Bella grew bigger and more adventurous, our weekends away came to an end because she was now exploring the world of her own garden and beyond. On one occasion, she tried to walk across our pond at Snowhill and was so surprised when she sank through the water lilies. She scrambled out and shook herself with the utmost dignity as if to say, "I meant to do that!"

One of her favourite adventures was to climb up on a high shelf in the garage. Then, very late one night, when we were all tucked up in bed, we were woken by a very strange noise coming from downstairs. It was a bit frightening, as it sounded like gasping and heavy breathing, so we got up to investigate, only to find Bella under the stairs with her face covered in blood! She had let herself out of the cat flap and had climbed up to sit on the high shelf in the garage. She must have nodded off to sleep in the dark and fallen onto the concrete floor, resulting in a broken jaw!! How terrible for her!

Of course, we did not know this, and it was the middle of the night, so we gently wrapped her up in a soft blanket, waited for dawn to break, and rushed her to the vet, where she stayed in their hospital for the next four days. The vet did a miraculous job mending her jaw, and Bella made a full recovery, living on to the ripe old age of just three weeks short of nineteen years.

Apart from hunting and presenting us with numerous field mice (some dead and others alive), Bella's favourite pastime was to sit on top of the tropical fish tank, enjoying the warmth, after which she would sit in front of it gazing at it as though it was her own personal television. It became fascinating for the family to watch her, as every now and again, she would grab at the tank with her front paws as though trying to catch the fish. The intriguing thing was that she only did this when a catfish was swimming past!

Over the years, her relationship with Fred became really good, and they became great pals, so much so that, when Fred passed on, Bella spent nearly six months looking for him, sitting in his special places, and also sitting on our laps. I visited the vet and suggested that we might get another cat for her. To our surprise, the answer was definitely NO. The reason was that Fred, a much bigger homely cat, had been the dominant one, always sitting on the settee or our laps, and as the vet said, it was now Bella's turn. How right she was! For the next eleven years, Bella ruled the roost and pinned us down to the settee, snoring away on our laps.

9 — Goldfish. My fishy friends

As we had created a large pond in our cottage garden, we were delighted to find a small formal one in our new garden when we moved house to live in the town—in addition to being nearer to shops, library, dentist, and doctor. We also had the benefit of trains running up to London from a station only a ten-minute walk away. I still live in that lovely house.

Our grandson, George, visited frequently and one day, while looking into the pond, he said, "Grandma, do you think we could have some pet goldfish?" I had, as remarked on, in the chapter about Bella, kept tropical fish indoors and had greatly enjoyed watching and caring for them. It therefore seemed a very attractive idea and it gave me great delight to reply, "Yes George".

So, within a short while, my two sons, my grandson, and I were in the car driving off to the pet shop.

Once there, we chose six medium-sized fish—three males and three females—and hurried back to put them into the pond. George did the 'launching' and, as he did so, named them all: Lily, Grace and Molly for the 'girls' and David, Henry and Samuel for the 'boys.

Every day, I fed them special flaked fish food from the pet shop and they became quite tame. Bella, who was getting to be an 'old lady' by then was very interested in them, but to my delight only wanted to sit on the edge of the pond and watch as they swam about. Her favourite activity was to lick up any of the fish flakes that had fallen out of my hand and in fact I think that was the main reason for taking up her seat on the edge of the pond.

One day, when buying food, the assistant mentioned that herons (big birds that swoop down on ponds and eat the goldfish), had nested nearby.

So, with this information I bought netting to go over the pond and a plastic life-sized heron to stand in it.

The idea was that the real herons would be scared off, seeing what they thought would be a rival bird, and leave mine alone. Sadly, however, this did not work and, one by one, all six of our goldfish disappeared!

My grandson, George, poured the fish into the pond.

I still have the plastic bird but have now filled the pond with water plants and transformed it into a 'bog garden'. I am glad to say that this has been a huge success, as the blackbirds and blue tits love to bathe in the shallow water above the plants, and it is a great attraction for dragon and damsel flies. It is also a valuable drinking supply for all the little creatures that live in our garden.

10 — Fritz, my Miniature Schnauzer

Well, as you can imagine, after ten glorious years with Fred and nearly nineteen lovely years with Bella, life was very empty. Both my sons had moved away from home, and my wonderful husband, Richard, had passed away. I was feeling very low, but I could not bring myself to acquire another cat as I felt I would always be comparing it to Fred and Bella.

As I was getting older, I wanted to keep as fit as possible and read a leaflet at home about walking, which appealed to me. So, I thought that maybe I should get a dog, which would need walking every day.

So, once I had made up my mind, I set out to find one that would suit me.

Initially, I thought I would get a 'rescue dog'—maybe a small one that needed a good home. But, on researching various dog homes I discovered that most of the dogs that needed re-homing were either very large Alsatians, huge Irish Wolfhounds, or the occasional very small dog that didn't need much walking.

Thus, I realised that, for me, obtaining a rescue dog was not going to be an option. I knew that I should be sensible and choose exactly what *was* suitable for me. I looked and looked, and asked around whenever I saw someone walking their dog. There were so many wonderful pets, but the only ones that *really* appealed to me were the Miniature Schnauzers! They were just the right size, looked beautiful, were very affectionate, and they didn't shed hairs; that was a real bonus!

Next came the job of finding one!

Intensive searching on the internet got more and more confusing, and the dogs seemed to become more and more expensive! It was extremely worrying as it became clear that there were a lot of so-called 'breeders' selling puppies at exorbitant prices.

At this time, another problem arose. It turned out to be extremely serious. It was new at the time, but now we all know it well. Covid! A serious, infectious virus that, one way or another, had a great effect on every person in the country. Indeed, the virus was spreading rapidly worldwide, and many countries, including the U.K., were going into a lockdown situation that lasted for some time.

It was a sad and lonely time for many people, and as things began to ease, it soon became evident that dogs were definitely "man's best friend," as there were so many more puppies out walking with their new owners.

One morning, coming home from shopping, right outside my house, there were two young men walking the most adorable miniature Schnauzer puppy right outside my house. I had to ask where they had acquired it, and they very kindly gave me the breeder's name. A dog like their puppy was exactly what I was after!

I didn't hesitate. I phoned immediately, only to be told that all her puppies had been sold. It was so disappointing, but just as I was saying goodbye, the lady said, "I have a friend who's also a Schnauzer breeder. I'll give you her contact number". Well, that turned out to be my lucky day, for not only was this new breeder the ex-President of the Kennel Club, but in her words, she was a breeder, NOT a 'greed'er!! As I have mentioned before, the prices of puppies on the internet were exorbitant, but this lady was really fair.

However, there was a snag. She told me that all her puppies were spoken for but that one prospective owner was unable to conclude the purchase. So, she would offer the dog to me if I could purchase it immediately. Of course, this arrangement meant that I had no choice of the puppies and had to take the one that was left. It was 'take it or leave it'.

She added that although I had said that I definitely wanted a puppy, if I did not like it when I saw it, I could walk away. Again, I felt that the breeder was being extremely fair when she told me about the circumstances and the good terms.

I fell in love with the little puppy as soon as I saw him. He was very handsome and was obviously a thoroughbred specimen. I agreed on the terms and we made the contract of sale there and then! I had definitely decided that this puppy was going to be mine!! And, shortly, he would be.

My very loving Miniature Schnauzer, "Fritz".

How exciting it was to realise, when I got home, that I had acquired my dog, and he would very soon be home with me.

Feeling great joy, I went to the local pet shop with a dear friend, where I purchased a puppy harness, lead, food, water bowls, a dog bed and a blanket.

Of course, my new puppy would need a toy—we chose a chewy toy squirrel who, because it was made to be a flat toy, we called "Road Kill".

Arrangements were worked out for Mark, my eldest son, to drive me from Sussex to Essex, where the kennels were located. With Mark driving, I could hold the puppy safely on my lap for the return journey.

Events were now moving at a pace as the breeder wanted all the puppies to go to their new homes over the coming weekend. It was a Friday and there was no time to do a bank transfer, so the breeder very reasonably asked for cash.

Thank goodness banks opened in those days on a Saturday morning, so I could draw out the cash—in a very large envelope.

Sunday morning soon came, and Mark and I sped off to Essex with a sense of great excitement mixed with trepidation at the thought that it could all go horribly wrong.

What if, on second viewing, I no longer liked the puppy?

Was I really being sensible handing over a large sum in bank notes (even though the price was very fair compared to all the other prices for puppies I had looked at) to someone unknown to me?

And so, I worried.

I am glad to be able to tell you that nothing could have been better than what actually happened. Usually, I would have done a lot more research, checking that all the information I had received was correct and bone-fide, but I would have lost the chance to buy my miniature Schnauzer puppy, as other buyers were interested, so I had to act quickly.

I felt lucky that I had been given the option to walk away on arrival at the kennels if I did not like the set-up or, indeed, the puppy that I was intending to buy. At this point, I did not know that the breeder was one of the top breeders in the world of miniature and standard Schnauzers, so when we walked into her home, we were taken aback to see rosettes pinned up all over her walls from her Crufts-winning show dogs.

What a discovery to find, by chance, the best breeder of Miniature Schnauzers from whom I could buy a puppy. I knew then that the deal was sealed, and all that there was left to do was to meet the puppy himself.

Mark and I were trying not to look too impressed as we were shown into a lounge with a large black leather sofa and extra-large dog beds, a table and chairs and two adult Schnauzers plus *two* tiny puppies.

Wow, I would never have dreamt that my search for a Miniature Schnauzer would turn out this way. As we played with the puppies, the breeder told us that the silver female was my puppy's mother, and the black one was his auntie. She then went out of the room to give us a cooling off period. At exactly that moment, the little girl dog got fed up and went back to her bed, whilst the boy, wagging his little tail, climbed all over our feet, wanting to be with us.

When the breeder returned, she was carrying a cream-coloured square of fake fur material with a pattern of brown paw prints. She then rubbed it all over both adults and the other puppy, finally giving it to me to wrap my puppy in. "This will help him to settle into his new home," she told us. "The scent will remind him of his mother and dog family."

She also passed over a large packet of puppy dog biscuits, which would be his staple food for the next eight months.

It was time to go home now, and as we passed by all the rosettes through the bungalow to the front door, I was already feeling an extremely proud new dog owner.

The last words from the breeder were, "Do you live in a house with stairs?" to which I replied, "Yes" Then you will have to get two stair gates, one for the top and one for the bottom, just in case he should manage to climb up them because he will only fall down them! Oh dear, one thing I had not thought of in my preparations for my new companion to come and live with me.

Tucked up in the back seat of the car with Mark driving at a sedate speed, we made the journey back to Sussex, and my little bundle of trembling fluff eventually settled in my lap, wrapped in the fur square, gazing up to the lighted streetlamps as it was now approaching evening. By this time, we had left the house in Snow Hill and had moved to a much larger home near the church in East Grinstead.

Once home, I found that I immediately had to make a decision about the stairs because halfway up there was a curving bend. The curve was comprised of three treads that were very narrow close to the bend's newel post, and extra wide on the opposite side of the staircase, close to the wall. It struck me that this could be rather dangerous for a very small puppy to navigate.

I devised a quick solution, which was to drape a dressing gown on the narrow part of the stair treads, thus obliging the little dog to pass down the wall side where the treads were wider and safer.

As it was all so new to this little puppy, venturing up the stairs didn't occur to him for some time.

Over the next few days both my sons and I tried to work out the best way of attaching the stair gates without disturbing my newly wallpapered hall. Then, a few days later, before we could solve this problem, I heard a little whimpering noise, only to find my puppy at the top of the stairs, looking helpless as to how to get down!

It seemed to me that the only thing to do was to show him. After just three attempts, he mastered it by sliding down each step on his tummy. The dressing gown had worked, keeping him on the safe side of the stair treads, so there was no need for a pair of difficult stair gates! It certainly showed us how smart he was going to be when he grew up.

Now was the time to make a definite decision on a name. The day that my friend and I had purchased the necessary bowls, bed, lead, and collar, I had impulsively told the shop assistant—when she inquired—that his name would be "Fritz". So, now he was actually here, Fritz it had to be.

Why I had chosen that name at the time, I do not know. Perhaps I had had in mind that he was a Schnauzer and Fritz was a good German name. Who knows? But the name has always suited him just fine and has informally transmuted to "Fritzy"!

As I have mentioned before, I purchased a very smart collar and lead so that when the time was ready, and after all his necessary vaccinations, we would be ready to venture out for a walk.

However, on our first few visits to the vet, while he was still very small, I carried Fritz tucked into a wicker shopping basket. This allowed him to see and witness passing people and cars so that he could get used to the hubbub of life outside the house—a kind of initiation into the 'big outdoors'.

Soon, Fritz was ready for his first walk, which was shared with my two sons, Mark and Alex, and my grandson, George. What horror when a car roared past just as we reached the pavement,

Fritz leapt into my neighbour's garden, landing in the middle of a small bush, and I was left with the lead and collar dangling in my hand! Thank goodness for the bush because there was little Fritz stuck in the middle of it, trembling with fright, and if it had not been there, I dread to think what might have happened.

As I write this, I think that the experience with the motor car must have affected poor Fritz deeply because, today, as an adult dog, he is still nervous about very loud noises, such as high-revving motorbikes roaring past in the street.

Thunderstorms also frighten him. On the other hand, perhaps this is common to most dogs. I guess that it is likely to be.

It was intended to be a family excursion as my two sons and grandson shared the new adventure of walking the puppy for the first time. However,

"Plan B", as they say, had suddenly materialised as we chanted, "This collar is not going to work." Retrieving Fritz, we all piled into the car and sped off to the pet shop, where a very helpful lady assistant measured him and fitted a sturdy-looking harness.

At the check-out desk, she asked if we had an identity tag fitted to his collar, to which we replied, "No!" only to be told, "It's the law, didn't you know."

Having heard about the incident involving the motorbike, she very kindly explained that by law, every dog needed to wear a tag engraved with a contact number in case the dog got lost or stolen.

Sadly, it was a time when popular breeds and pedigree dogs were being stolen and sold on the internet because of the high demand for them. So, she concluded with, "Don't put your name or the dog's name on the tag, as this makes it much easier for thieves."

We chose a bone-shaped tag, and after only ten minutes for engraving, we all walked back to the car with Fritz wearing his harness and sporting a brand-new shiny tag attached to his collar. Now, we were safe to walk every day and explore most of East Grinstead and surrounding areas. There were many exciting new walks for Fritz in the vicinity of our house.

In particular, there was a lovely mansion house now belonging to the Local Council with extensive grounds open to the public, and they are very popular with dog walkers.

One day, on my walk with Fritz, we met a small group of people chatting, with their dogs playing and running around them—all off their leads. On our approach, they said 'hello' and introduced themselves while asking about Fritz.

Then, to my fear, they suggested that I let Fritz off his lead so that he could join in. At first, I was really nervous, remembering that the breeder had told me not to do this for fear of him being stolen as he was a thoroughbred. Eventually, as they all explained, it was safer to let him play with other dogs who all came back when called, and I could see how much he wanted to join in. I agreed.

Oh, what fun they all had. Following the other dogs' example, dear little Fritz came running back to me--- what a relief! As we parted, it was agreed that we would all try to make the same time as many days as possible, and hence, a real friendship between the dogs grew. Real bonding was taking place as we all met up over the months ahead.

In fact, we still meet even now. 'Olive' is a Jack Russel, 'Poppy' is a Cavapoo, 'Misty' is a Bedlington, and 'Teddy' is a Yorkshire Terrier. I was also doing well with new friends Lorraine, Russell, Roland, and Sophia, all with dogs and all of us putting the world to rights as we chatted, with the dogs chasing and playing around us.

So much for my many walks with my dog, but I didn't mind a bit when I saw his joy in spending time with his doggy companions.

I had observed that the other dogs were all wearing harnesses, and Fritz was getting on well with his, having now learnt to lift his paws up one at a time when putting it on. The harness also made it much easier to attach the lead when the dogs came back.

Another sure-fire trick to train the dogs to return to us was a 'treat' that all the owners, me included, had in our pockets. So that none got left out, it was agreed that on command, all the dogs would "SIT" and each be given its treat in turn.

What a picture it was to see these five furry friends sitting and waiting. And what a great achievement for us owners to know that they all understood these two important commands of "Wait" and "Sit" that could very well help them in the future on important occasions. Indeed, it took me back to the long-ago day when my dear pet, Pepé, saved his own life by 'sitting' when I shouted to him before he was run over, safely, by a car! I was so glad that I had trained him. And now, Fritz was being successfully trained to do the same thing.

Fritz wasn't the only new thing I acquired at that time. I met a new 'man in my life', who became my permanent partner. Now, having been on my own for eight years, we were a family of three! Wonderful!

Fritz was a fast learner and very keen to 'have a go' at anything new, so when Peter suggested we might teach him to use the cat flap that was already in the door going out into the garden, I said, "We can try, but it probably won't work." Well, how wrong

I was as Peter, with great patience, tied the cat flap open and encouraged Fritz to climb through, which he did quite happily. The next thing was to get him to push it open with his nose. At first, he sniffed and then pushed gently, not managing to open the flap more than a crack. But with great encouragement from Peter, the crack got wider and wider and, eventually, out through the flap, Fritz went into the garden.

Coming back was now an issue because he had only used the flap for going out, and at first, he wouldn't push it inwards. But, when a bowl of food was placed on the floor inside, bingo! he was through.

What a difference it has made to our lives. Now Fritz is in and out of our garden whenever he pleases. That is especially good because, although he is house-trained, he often needs a night-time visit to the garden, and poor Peter used to have to get up during the night to let him out and back in when he barked to us. No longer!

A few weeks later, I had a telephone call from a neighbour asking if I knew Fritz was sniffing around in her garden two gardens away from ours. My reply was, "No, and I have no idea how he could have got in there!"

Armed with his harness and lead, I went to collect him and try to find out how he had arrived there.

When my neighbour mentioned the 'hedgehog hole' in her fence, the penny dropped as I recalled the hedgehog hole in my fence and also the one in our adjoining middle neighbour's garden. We had not bargained for the fact that by now Fritz had the confidence to climb through small holes, plus he has the inquiring nature that all schnauzers seem to have; he was up for any adventure, and finding a new hole, he was through and off to the next one.

Thank goodness the holes only linked our three gardens, and sadly, there have not been any sightings of hedgehogs for many years. So, Peter blocked our hole up securely, knowing that once found, Fritz would be certain to use it again.

Fritz was now growing, and at the monthly check-ups with the vet, he was right on target for his breed to be 8.5 kilos when fully grown. This monthly programme of monitoring the first year of a puppy's life is very reassuring for an owner. It builds confidence in the dogs to get used to visiting the surgery. In fact, Fritz really enjoyed them, as not only was there a treat given during the visit, but there was a chance to meet other dogs and also be patted by the vets and told how handsome he is.

As Fritz grew, so did his fur, which created the next task of finding a groomer. So, I booked him in at a local dog parlour. It was terrible! He came out crudely shorn and without his lovely Schnauzer eyebrows and beard. He looked awful.

One day, in the park, a beautiful, magnificently trimmed white poodle turned up. He was called "Bobby". After a quick 'hello', I enquired of the owner where she took him to be clipped.

Armed with that valuable information, I made an appointment as soon as possible. Our new groomer is a fifteen-minute drive away, but she is superb. She has been trained to undertake the classic Schnauzer style. You can imagine that she is a busy 'stylist', and we book him in with her at five-week intervals, several visits in advance. The result of this lucky 'find' is that Fritz looks like a champion Schnauzer and is constantly being admired by women and men alike. Indeed, when I asked his breeder for a pedigree chart, it turned out that he has *six* Crufts champions in his six-generation pedigree! Wow!

Fritz is now three years old, and we are having such a lot of incredible adventures together. So many, in fact, that I am going to leave them for another storybook for you to read and enjoy, just about him.

THE END

A final word for you from Angela.

Dear reader,

I really hope that you have enjoyed reading this book about my wonderful pets as much as I have enjoyed writing about them. Thank you for reading my book. It means a lot to me.

If any of you would like to write to me, sharing your own dear animal stories, please do so through the publishers:

angela@impartopublishing.com

I shall be sure to read your emails and reply to you.

THIS IS A SPACE TO DRAW AND COLOUR IN YOUR OWN LOVING PETS.

THIS IS A SPACE TO DRAW AND COLOUR IN YOUR OWN LOVING PETS.

www.ingramcontent.com/pod-product-compliance
Lightning Source LLC
Chambersburg PA
CBHW071712040426
42446CB00011B/2025